Editor-in-Chief and Founder:
  Lyndon H. LaRouche, Jr.
Editorial Board: *Lyndon H. LaRouche, Jr. , Helga
  Zepp-LaRouche, Robert Ingraham, Tony
  Papert, Gerald Rose, Dennis Small, Jeffrey
  Steinberg, William Wertz*
Co-Editors: *Robert Ingraham, Tony Papert*
Managing Editor: *Nancy Spannaus*
Technology: *Marsha Freeman*
Books: *Katherine Notley*
Ebooks: *Richard Burden*
Graphics: *Alan Yue*
Photos: *Stuart Lewis*
Circulation Manager: *Stanley Ezrol*

INTELLIGENCE DIRECTORS
Counterintelligence: *Jeffrey Steinberg, Michele
  Steinberg*
Economics: *John Hoefle, Marcia Merry Baker,
  Paul Gallagher*
History: *Anton Chaitkin*
Ibero-America: *Dennis Small*
Russia and Eastern Europe: *Rachel Douglas*
United States: *Debra Freeman*

INTERNATIONAL BUREAUS
Bogotá: *Miriam Redondo*
Berlin: *Rainer Apel*
Copenhagen: *Tom Gillesberg*
Houston: *Harley Schlanger*
Lima: *Sara Madueño*
Melbourne: *Robert Barwick*
Mexico City: *Gerardo Castilleja Chávez*
New Delhi: *Ramtanu Maitra*
Paris: *Christine Bierre*
Stockholm: *Ulf Sandmark*
United Nations, N.Y.C.: *Leni Rubinstein*
Washington, D.C.: *William Jones*
Wiesbaden: *Göran Haglund*

ON THE WEB
e-mail: eirns@larouchepub.com
www.larouchepub.com
www.executiveintelligencereview.com
www.larouchepub.com/eiw
Webmaster: *John Sigerson*
Assistant Webmaster: *George Hollis*
Editor, Arabic-language edition: *Hussein Askary*

EIR (ISSN 0273-6314) *is published weekly
(50 issues), by EIR News Service, Inc.,
P.O. Box 17390, Washington, D.C. 20041-0390.
(703) 777-9451*

European Headquarters: E.I.R. GmbH, Postfach
Bahnstrasse 9a, D-65205, Wiesbaden, Germany
Tel: 49-611-73650
Homepage: http://www.eirna.com
e-mail: eirna@eirna.com
Director: Georg Neudecker

Montreal, Canada: 514-461-1557

Denmark: EIR - Danmark, Sankt Knuds Vej 11,
basement left, DK-1903 Frederiksberg, Denmark.
Tel.: +45 35 43 60 40, Fax: +45 35 43 87 57. e-mail:
eirdk@hotmail.com.

Mexico City: EIR, Sor Juana Inés de la Cruz 242-2
Col. Agricultura C.P. 11360
Delegación M. Hidalgo, México D.F.
Tel. (5525) 5318-2301
eirmexico@gmail.com

Canada Post Publication Sales Agreement
#40683579

Postmaster: Send all address changes to *EIR*, P.O.
Box 17390, Washington, D.C. 20041-0390.

Signed articles in *EIR* represent the views of the
authors, and not necessarily those of the Editorial
Board.

Kesha Rogers: To Save the U.S. Economy, Revive the Space Program

Editorial

by Kesha Rogers of Texas, a Leader of the LaRouche PAC Policy Committee

It's in the DNA of our country to explore, and we must never stop doing this;
we must lead, we must learn, and we must discover.

—Astronaut Scott Kelly

Scott Kelly is absolutely right! It is in our cultural DNA to explore! It is in the DNA of every human being to explore. This is the creative nature that is unique only to the human species, the only species that can create new scientific breakthroughs, the only species that can conquer space.

Now the United States faces a critical decision which will determine the future of our nation. Will we continue to go along with the dying policy of the trans-Atlantic system, which is a policy of death for our U.S. economy at the hands of the bankrupt Wall Street financial institutions and the destructive policies of the last four terms of the Bush and Obama Administrations? Or, will we restore a national mission and vision for the future of our nation, to once again lead the world in scientific and economic progress? We have to lift our nation once more out of the depths of despair. It is urgent that we revive a scientific mission, if we are to restart the economic progress of our nation again. This must be done in cooperation with the effort being led by the nations of Russia and China, as leaders of the BRICS nations, to bring about a new "win-win" paradigm for the direction of mankind on the planet. The greatest tool that we have in the United States for bringing about that renewed mission and renewed optimism for our nation, is fully launching a revival of our national space program, with all its irreplaceable contributions to scientific and economic progress.

In a discussion with activists on March 10, Lyndon LaRouche declared, "The space program has been the basis for all competent economic policy. It is something that Obama shut down, and destroyed the possibility to organize the economy." He elaborated further, "We need a scientific program based on scientifically quali-

fied principles. The only way to save the U.S. economy is with the space program. Put the people back to work. Get rid of Obama and the Bush family, and let's get back to rebuilding the United States."

This fight and mission, to revive our space program, is one in which I have continued to lead. In 2010, I launched a national campaign for U.S. Congress to denounce the egregious attacks on our space program, the cuts to manned space program, and the canceling of Constellation by President Obama. This was one of the greatest wrongs done to our nation by any President, because he shut down the basis of our ability to improve our relationship with our solar system.

This is a policy that must now be reversed, or the United States may never recover again. Today, faced with a worse than useless slate of Presidential pre-election candidates, I have re-launched that initiative on an even broader level, to change the subject of policy discussion and debate, and restore a national mission centered around putting our space program at the forefront of our national agenda.

Over the last few weeks, in expanding on these efforts, I have held events and attended meetings to organize some of the best scientific and most-skilled minds of our nation,— who have been instrumental in the building of our manned space program at Johnson Space Center,— to recognize that what we are fighting for is nothing less than the future of our nation. Through these interventions, a growing cadre of qualified scientists, engineers, and astronauts are beginning to do more than reminisce on the old glory days, or lament today's lack of leadership and budgets; they are beginning to use their scientific authority to define what our future must be. With this, we have witnessed a renewed optimism, and new willingness to speak up.

Visionary Leadership

It has always been the creative nature of mankind to explore new horizons and to create new frontiers. But the cause of exploring and conquering space, presents to man a whole new set of questions and new challenges that must be solved. The first step to solving the challenges of understanding man as man in the universe, starts with vision. Our space program would not have witnessed the great breakthroughs it has afforded to us, increasing the progress of mankind, if it had not been for the creative imagination of great visionaries and pioneers of space. Yet the pioneers of rocketry and space flight knew that their ideas would never even come close to being realized without a leader with vision. Our nation's leaders who had vision, who understood that human progress starts by removing all limitation to growth, have been few and far between. Great visionaries understood that where there was no vision, the people would perish.

President John F. Kennedy was a brilliant example of true leadership with vision. President Kennedy was inspired by the efforts of great leaders like President Franklin Roosevelt and Abraham Lincoln, whose American system tradition he adhered to. It was under the leadership of Lincoln with the development of the trans-continental railway system, and Franklin Roosevelt's Tennessee Valley Authority (TVA), that our nation saw some of its greatest economic progress. Now Kennedy had a unique opportunity to put the United States back on the map toward greatness, and lead the world in the drive for developing space. The vision for the space program that Kennedy set out for the nation was one that would transform our economic progress in virtually every field. This did not happen without a fight, but what Kennedy showed, like Lincoln and FDR, was that we could take the most desperate and economically-collapsed areas of our nation and turn them into productive machines. This is why President Kennedy's announcement that we would land a man on the Moon and return him safely to earth before the end of the decade, was not just a short term thrill or merely the effort to come in first in a space race, but would prove instrumental to the economic progress of the nation.

Kennedy understood that it was not just the destiny our nation to go to the Moon, but, as all the great pioneers of space have taught us, it was our destiny to conquer and terraform all of space for the progress of all mankind.

These words expressed by President Kennedy in his famous Rice University speech, given in Houston, Texas, on Sept. 12, 1962, make clear Kennedy's promotion of the true cause of mankind in conquering space.

We set sail on this new sea because there is new knowledge to be gained, and new rights to be won, and they must be won and used for the progress of all people.

We choose to go to the Moon in this decade and do the other things, not because they are easy, but because they are hard, because that goal will serve to organize and measure the best of our energies and skills, because that challenge is one that we are willing to accept, one we are unwilling to postpone, and one which we intend to win, and the others, too.

Today, our nation is left void of a real vision, and of competent leadership acting for the future. We, the American people, must demand a return to sanity now. The space program once again stands as the only viable solution for pulling the United States out of the depths of death and despair, and reviving the greatest talents and minds of our nation. We must take these great resources of mind and put them to work again in restoring the physical and economic progress of the country, just as we did under the leadership of Presidents Lincoln, Franklin Roosevelt, and Kennedy. We require a vision and true leadership, to inspire the people of our nation, and to once again inspire the world. This effort will not be achieved by the United States alone, but only through abandoning the dead corpse of the trans-Atlantic system, run by a ruinous British empire and its destructive puppet in the White house, Obama. We must join with nations like Russia, India, and especially China, to bring about a renewed mission, putting an end to the political and economic strife by turning our eyes to the common aims of mankind, by developing mankind's understanding of the universe in which we live, through the development of space. Where shall we take our minds? The Chinese are leading the charge... to the far side of the Moon!

EIR Contents

www.larouchepub.com Volume 43, Number 12, March 18, 2016

Cover
This Week

*Ed White
performs first
U.S. spacewalk*

Creative Commons

I. New World Coming Into Being

The New Concept of the Nation for Mankind

Edited excerpts from Lyndon LaRouche's Fireside Chat of March 10.

Host John Ascher: The questions we've gotten, Lyn, are that people want to know if there is going to be an election this November? Are the candidates we're seeing now going to be the ones we're going to end up choosing between? What is your view in terms of where this so-called election process right now is heading? That's what is being asked by several people.

Lyndon LaRouche: I would say that in the United States right now, to the degree that some of us contribute new insights into what the United States can become, that we have to have a process of freedom. Because the problem is that the people who don't like us, who don't like freedom are the problem. But the question, then, therefore, is what is freedom? Some people say, "my idea of freedom is this" and their idea of freedom is not that.

So the point is, there has to be a coherence, an agreement, based on rational insight into practice. This is what has always worked in nations. This is what destroyed nations! Napoleon destroyed nations! The British always destroyed nations!

Ministry of Culture and Tourism, Republic of Turkey

Turkey's current President, Recep Tayyip Erdogan, is a puppet of the same British imperial forces that Turkish nationalists have historically sought to defeat. Here, Mustafa Kemal, called Atatürk, "father of the Turks," President of Turkey 1923-1938, and his wife Latife Uşalakizâde, in 1923.

They specialize in that; and this has been true too much in history.

So what you have, is you find that the formation of government is based on the *destruction* of separate governments, in conflict, the murder. I think of what Turkey is doing now, the dictatorship of Turkey. Now, this is not a characteristic of the Turks; this is not a characteristic, because I know something about the Turks and their history. I've been closely associated with some of the heroes in Turkey. And similar things are true of other nations. There is no reason why we should say that there is a natural hatred, a natural conflict among people in the world! It's not natural. The fact of the conflict is often an *un*natural product.

Because when people see what good is, when the *human being sees what good is*, in practice, you find that they do not want to do the kinds of things that the tyrants would like to produce. The question is, the arguments come, over what should be the good? What is the thing we should do which is good? What is better? And that's it.

And these other things are nonsense.

Where are we now, for example? Just to interrupt myself. Where are we now? We're on the edge of a gen-

China Manned Space Engineering Office

China is looking at the back side of the Moon. China is mobilizing itself for the next two generations for this mission and beyond. Here, an artist's conception of the core module of the Chinese large modular space station to be launched into low Earth orbit in 2018. Two laboratory modules will follow in 2020 and 2022.

eral thermonuclear war throughout the whole planet, and beyond the planet as such. And this thing that can happen right now in the kind of war which is being planned *right now*, can destroy the entire planet, and the planet's people, right now! And therefore, the question is, how do we prevent that from happening? And how do we do it without going into some kind of submission to this, or submission to that? No! It has to come from an *insight* into what truth is, what mankind is, what mankind must be. And a great number of people like,— I think you could say that Putin is a pretty good example of a model, is trying to do exactly that. And there are people in other parts of the world who are intent on doing that.

And that's what we have to do. We are seeing this thing with China, with Russia, with other parts of the planet now. We see these national units are coming into a convergence which is not just dropping into bed with each other, but it's a process of realizing that they have to work their way through something by which their common interests are furthered, in a willful and progressive way.

And that's what we're trying to do. You look at what China's doing. India's trying to work its way through

there. Other parts of the world are trying to work through that process. It's that kind of goal, that kind of process—and what it comes to, is when you come and start talking about the space program. You talk about the back side of the Moon.

Now, what's China doing? China is looking at the back side of the Moon, and the back side of the Moon is what China is trying to solve: What is the real meaning of this thing, the back side of the Moon? And China is mobilizing itself for the next two generations for just that purpose. And that's not just a purpose, but it's a beginning place to understand how mankind, Earthling mankind, can play a role in shaping the Galaxy. And the galaxy is the goal which mankind should be looking at right now.

Sins of the Fathers

Question: Good evening Lyn and all, this is J— from Michigan. The quality of questions presented to you and your responses over these past ten months, as I've told you before, has constantly been improving. And I was wondering if you could make some comments as to how we can all improve on our abilities to get through to others, whether they're ignorant of so much, or whether they're really knowledgeable about so much, so that we can constantly improve our ways of organizing people to change their ways of thinking. Please.

LaRouche: Well, the problem of changing people's way of thinking, has some competence to it. What should you really be concerned with is the development of the power of the individual person within the society as a framework, to influence that society in such a way that there is actual progress.

For example, Einstein. Einstein is a paragon, a model, for what the purpose of mankind *is*; and if you understand Einstein, you want to understand what Einstein was, what he was doing, what his achievements were, what he opposed, as opposed to all the other people who were fools, relatively. I mean, most of the scientists who were associated with Einstein's name were actually foolish because they had a gimmick. And you know, we just had this recent experience to remind people that Einstein had discovered something and they hadn't been able to hear it and recognize its existence for their entire life. [laughs]

And the point is, there are individual people who have a yen, shall we say, for achievement of the goals of mankind. You think about the goal of mankind, it's like the soul of mankind. And guiding the soul of mankind is what's actually is a pretty good efficient representation of what Einstein was. Einstein was a *very good soul*, and a rare model of a good soul.

And that's what you have to go with. You have to look at yourself as a creative force for mankind, and that means you have obligations to make discoveries that mankind needs to discover.

Question: In the past few weeks, you have touched on the subject of the Electoral College, in terms of how Presidents seem to be selected, as opposed to elected. Can you give us a little more detail on your take on the current system with the Electoral College?

LaRouche: I think so, because, I have a sense of how the human mind works. And that's the only way we can really test these kinds of matters.

You have to recognize that mankind has to be a progressive creature. Mankind must create something fresh, to add something to what mankind should have done earlier. And that's the basis on which you have to operate. I mean, what do you think I do? I've been spending most of my time, my life, in terms of science, physical science, and the application of physical science.

And what do I worry about? I worry about the need for progress in physical science, and what the implications are of that. I've spent most of my life on that subject, and I've fought political forces in my life, especially my adult life,— I fought forces of that nature, and I enjoy doing that. Because in doing that, by enjoying it, you're saying, "well, this is pretty good. This is a nice thing! And the other stuff, nah, that's not nice stuff."

So I operate on that basis. I think it's a natural way that people should. I look at the history of my own family, which goes back quite some time, and I see what in my family were failures, but I see also what are successes, where my ancestors contributed something directly and explicitly to the betterment of mankind. And sometimes they did it in a funny way. I had a Scots-

man there who was a great killer, and he helped to fight the Civil War for the United States; but he was a Scotsman and he was a killer. Despite all those things, he was useful for that particular purpose. And so I've gone through that kind of process, and when you look at a lot of ancestors, as I've looked at a lot of ancestors, and you say what makes an ancestor good as opposed to being bad? And therefore you say: Well, I got this guy, and he's a problematic person to deal with. Like for example, I had two brothers, Scotsmen, and they were both very experienced in the Civil War period. One was a seaman and leading shipmate; and the other one was his brother who was a professional warrior. And he headed up a unit in the war. People like that.

So when you have families like that and you view them from that standpoint, you judge them based on, "yes, that was good, this was not so nice; this was good," and so forth.

So the way you have to live in life is, you have to think about people who you have been part of in the making of them, and you have to be critical of how do we judge them? What was the merit of what they did? What were the weaknesses and failures of what they did? And therefore, you look at yourself in that context, and you say, "this is what I must do, and this is what I must not do."

And that's the only way we can really efficiently solve these problems or questions. If you cannot be critical of yourself, if you can't be critical about your own ancestors or simply the people you know, the people you work with, if you don't have a good insight into the virtues and failures of these people, you cannot come up with a real social context. It just can't happen. And for every human being, particularly for anyone,— you know, I've been a significant figure at certain times of my life, and my self-criticism powers are rather good; but I wouldn't like to do anything that was not good. And so that's what you have to live with.

And if you can live that way,— because you don't have any map that tells you that everything is power, and everything defines what makes good or bad,— you don't get it that way! Mankind is always changing mankind. Or that's what the purpose is: Mankind must always change mankind. But how? By recognizing that there's something they should have done, but didn't; or something they shouldn't have done, for example. And that standard, and the desire to create something new and fresh to mankind is the real purpose of life to any person, who—I mean, with my devotion that's all I'm concerned about. What I always have been concerned about is that kind of issue: What is good, and what do I have to do to improve myself so I can do something which is more good? And that's the only way you can function.

You can't function on some abstract value. You have to have the desire to do something better than was done before, and you have to do it zealously.

Their 'Guilt Streak'

Question: Hey, Lyn, this is R— from Texas. I'm just curious: What is the jokesters' endgame and what you think their end goal is in this whole situation? I'm just curious.

LaRouche: I think they want to be teased by something which is not real. They want to believe in it hard, if possible. And they want to say "I'm perfect." Which we know is not true!

But we can get people to become better! If we can tempt them to do something where they can look at themselves and see themselves in a better light in their life, that's something that is very good. It's the best you get in most circles. You don't get good people as such; you get people who wish they were good people. That's your best shot!

Question: I just want to run something by you that happened, that you might get a little charge out of: I was in a pizza shop after school the other day and there were two women who were discussing the election. And both women were lamenting the fact that they didn't know who to vote for; they were talking about choosing the "better of two evils" and we've gone through that situation before. It's interesting that they called Trump a "bully," and a few other not so nice names; and then they cited Hillary as untrustworthy. And they said Bernie was a flip-flopper and he would only win by default, which was kind of interesting.

And the word "untrustworthy" is actually my word. What they really said was that "Hillary is a lyin' ho."

So, I say, "Oh, OK, ladies, what do you think about the election? I was just listening, and I overheard what you were saying." And to my surprise, one of the

Creative Commons/Gage Skidmore

"So when they said 'Hillary is a lyin' ho,' I said, OK! After we laughed, I jumped into their conversation." Here, Hillary Clinton tells another whopper at a town hall meeting in Manchester, N.H. in January 2016.

women said, "somebody new is going to come into these elections. I really believe that. I think we're going to be surprised by someone entering this campaign who really deserves to be President, who really should be President. And people really think we're stupid, but I believe that. I told my kids that."

And I said, "OK, that's very interesting. I think you need to come to a meeting on Saturday. And I'm going to give you my information and you're going to give me your information, and I'm going to remind you and give you the address and we'll get together when you come to that meeting." And they were thinking, "Okay! what's this about?" and I was telling them, "just what we were talking about, how there *is* a new situation going on right now. There is a *positive* situation called the BRICS nations, and you need to learn about that. And you're absolutely right: someone is going to come into this election and it will be a surprise. And they are going to be the right person. And we are going to bring that about."

LaRouche: The key thing is when you have the insight, and this is the problem. The next step is to recognize what you can do to solve the problem. In other words, you see something, you experience something, you experience it and you say, "this is wrong." Or you say, "I've got to do something about this. I've got to influence them." And then you go to another state, "but I don't think they will actually respond," the way you want them to respond, and that's true. So how do we deal with that? And you have to really get closer to the inside of them to find out what is inside them, which is their guilt streak. And when the guilt streak really hits them,

kremlin.ru

"There is a positive *situation called the BRICS nations, and you need to learn about that." Here, presidents Vladimir Putin of Russia, Jacob Zuma of South Africa, and Xi Jinping of China at the Fifth BRICS Summit in Durban, South Africa, March 2013.*

they're going to be very serious about what they do with their life. So that's the best answer I think we can give. Because most people waste their lives, in just that way.

Ascher: OK, Lyn, we have a question from a gentleman named R—. He wanted you to talk about "how we can end the private Federal Reserve run out of the one square mile City of London Corporation," and go back to U.S. Treasury issue. And he says, "We need to join an international movement to end private central banks. How about canceling all the fraudulent and criminal private debt." That's what he's asking about, what to do about all this unpayable debt?

Our Mission-Orientation

LaRouche: Well, obviously if the debt is unpayable, it's unpayable, isn't it? And therefore, what are you doing bothering with that stuff? [laughter]

The point is, the debt has to be a necessary debt, otherwise it doesn't work. Now, what's a necessary debt? Well, the necessary debt is an obligation which some people accept from other people. What does that mean? That means, you say, "this is something which mankind needs as a species, mankind needs this contribution, mankind needs this support; mankind needs this stimulus to see these kinds of options." But this requires a

certain insight into the people you're looking into. What're you going to do about it? How is it going to work? How can you move them?

And I say, in most cases, the people who will try to do something in that direction will often find themselves frustrated because they haven't found out what the secret is, or because the person they're looking at hasn't recognized what the secret is, either.

And so therefore, what we're doing now, right now, is the space program. The space program is activated in southern Texas, the Texas area. And it's done by people who are associated with me. These people who are associated with me, happen to be radiating their approach to the same subject. They're attracted to this; this is real. Yes, this is something that we're doing, it was taken away from us. Obama took it away from us! We had a space program, we were solving the problems of man's role in space. And Obama came along and shut it down! And Texas suffered in particular. Because the people in Texas who were involved in this were among the most highly qualified people of all, a category of people who were greatly creative people!

Now we've rescued a few of those people who were pushed off by Obama, who pushed them off from their career, their achievement,— wasted them, wasted parts of their lives. And now we've got a chance to get back there and get that thing moving. It's not as good as it had been when Obama shut it down, but the best thing we can do is shut Obama down! And open the gates for success. And you've got the whole area, that whole area of Texas which has people who are affected by that particular legacy. And that's what you start from. That's what we're doing, starting from, again, in trying to get a refresher of what had been the original space program. We're working on the basis of people we knew, who were the leaders of the space program.

And therefore it's simply saying, we want to do the job. Well, here's how we were doing the job and it's important that we continue the job, so let's do it. You'll

LaRouche: What we're doing right now is the space program. People associated with me are radiating their approach to it. Yes, this is something that we're doing. It was taken away from us. Obama took it away from us!

The scientific concepts of biogeochemist Vladimir Vernadsky— the initiator of the idea of the Biosphere— whose concept of the "Noösphere," has been cited and further developed by Lyndon LaRouche.

save a lot of lives and a lot of minds just by doing that. So, I think the idea of going to the space program is really the way to see the *real future* of mankind.

Ascher: Well, that brings us to the end here of our allotted time, Lyn. I think you hit on some very important things in your last discussion. I wanted to see if you had any concluding remarks here?

LaRouche: We have to take a mission orientation as our directive. We have to assess what are the things that we have to do which are accessible to us to do, and to start doing it! And I think that the space program—because the space program is so important—is the most important thing that mankind has to deal with right now. So the space program is needed. We have a few people who are fresh at it; we have some people who will become drawn into it, we're going to fight for it, and it's going to be good. It'll be good for us, why? Because it makes us feel good about ourselves.

Ascher: OK! That gives everybody an orientation. I'd like to thank you again, Lyn, for our discussion here this evening. And that concludes this Fireside Chat. Good evening, Lyn.

LaRouche: Thank you! Have fun!

Asia's Fast North-South Access To Europe Is Almost Ready

by Ramtanu Maitra

For purposes of trade, Asia's access to Europe, and Europe's access to Asia, for almost 150 years, has primarily been by sea through the Suez Canal, once that Canal was opened in 1869. Over these years, Asia's economy has grown many times over and so has Europe's. This trade route has long been overburdened and can be expected to remain so, even with its newly increased capacity. Moreover, most Asian, and all South Asian countries situated east of Pakistan, could trade with Central Asia only through Europe or China. These countries have had to depend on a land route through China and the long sea route through Europe via Rotterdam and St. Petersburg. Both routes are long and hence expensive and time consuming.

This difficulty gave birth to the concept of the International North-South Transport Corridor (INSTC), just as the other, East-West features of the World Land-Bridge were also in gestation. The INSTC is a multi-modal transportation route officially agreed upon in 2000 by Iran, Russia, and India at a meeting in St. Petersburg. Eleven nations have joined since then, from Belarus to Syria to Kyrgyzstan. This corridor is designed to link South Asia and the west coast ports of some Southeast Asian nations to Europe and Central Asia, via the Indian Ocean and Persian Gulf to the Caspian Sea, running through Iran and Azerbaijan and then through the Russian Federation to northern Europe.

The Delay

The route is not yet complete. However, on the recommendation of the fifth INSTC Coordination Council meeting held in Baku, Azerbaijan in 2013, a dry run of INSTC was successfully conducted by the Federation of Freight Forwarders of India in 2014 on the routes, (1) Nhava Sheva (Mumbai, India)-Bandar Abbas (Iran)-Tehran-Bandar Anzali (Iran)-Astrakhan (Russia), and (2) Nhava Sheva-Bandar Abbas-Baku (Azerbaijan).

As of now, Asian freight traveling via the INSTC unloads at Bandar Abbas on the Persian Gulf and then travels by rail to Qazvin (Iran); then by road to Bandar Anzali, to be loaded onto a ship crossing the Caspian Sea (south to north), and is then unloaded at Astrakhan in the Russian Federation (**Route 2** on the map). From Astrakhan, the cargo will become rail freight traveling to northern Europe. That is where it stands now. Within three years, however, this will all change.

The reasons behind the delay in developing this trade route have been many. Iran was under severe sanctions crippling its economy, Russia was in political disarray, and India was still very inward looking, making little effort to enhance its trade linkages. The situation now is dramatically different, and the demands and capabilities of all those countries through which this multi-modal trade route winds its way to Europe, have increased immensely. Moreover, the Suez Canal route, despite its increased capacity, is still going to be busy and is still the longer and more time-consuming route and, as a result, more expensive.

Because of the difficulties stated above, the INSTC has yet to be fully developed. However, now that Iran has been unshackled from sanctions, the INSTC is scheduled to be ready in 2019. The difficult part in the INSTC land route is the combined unloading and reloading, which now occurs a number of times between Qazvin, Bandar Anzali, and Astrakhan. This wastes time and money. This bottleneck will be removed when Iran builds the railroad from Qazvin to Rasht, through a mountain pass, to bring the trade route to the southwestern corner of the Caspian Sea, and then extends it along the western shore of the Caspian Sea to Astara, bordering Azerbaijan (**Route 3** on the map). Once the line reaches Astara, it will be linked to the existing Azerbaijan-Russian Federation railroad through Baku in Azerbaijan.

The good news is that the railroad has been given the proverbial green light by the head of Iranian Railways, Mohsen Pour Seyed Aghaie. On Jan. 12, 2016, *Trend News Agency* reported Aghaie as saying that "the construction of the Rasht-Astara railway will begin in 2016 and finish in 2019." The Qazvin-Rasht part of the line will be completed in 2017.

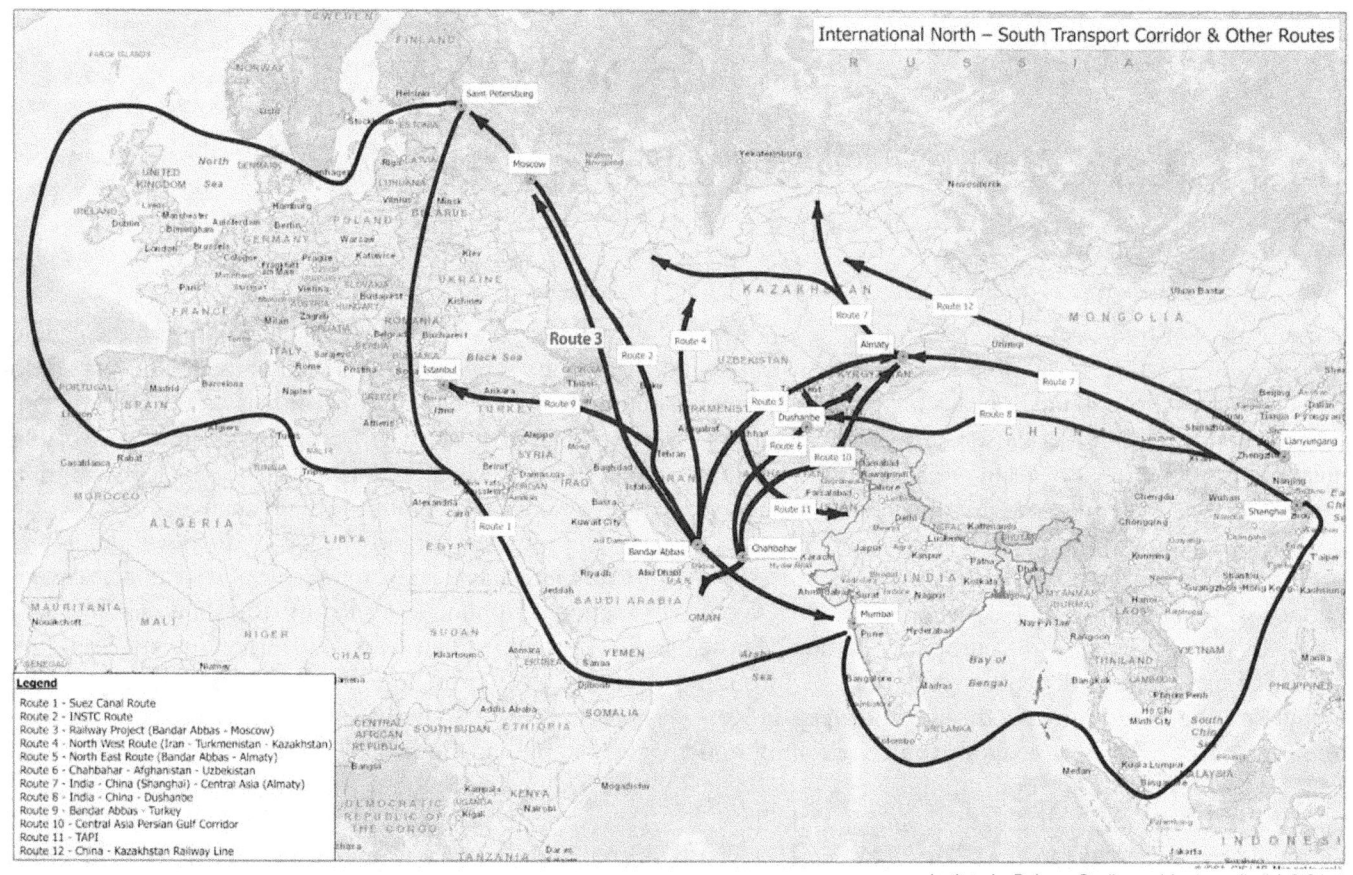

The International North-South Transport Corridor (INSTC), to be completed in 2019, will greatly increase efficiency and speed in moving container freight between points along a Mumbai-St. Petersburg axis, shown as Route 3. The INSTC is seen here in the context of other routes.

Iran Prioritizes

In the same *Trend News Agency* report, Aghaie is also quoted as saying, "The implementation of the railway project Qazvin-Rasht-Astara requires an investment of $1.5 billion. But this project is a priority for the Iranian government, and we will ensure the necessary funds." He added, "development of cargo transportation could give momentum to global economic recovery." In 2015, railway companies of Iran, Azerbaijan, and Russia signed a document to expedite construction of the 75 km Qazvin-Rasht-Astara segment.

The INSTC Coordination Council also plans to develop some important spurs. One such already in place is the 930 km rail link running from Uzen in oil- and gas-rich western Kazakstan through Turkmenistan to the existing railroad in Gorgan, northwestern Iran, running close to the southeastern coast of the Caspian Sea (**Route 4** on the map). This link, flagged off in December 2014, links Iran and Turkmenistan

with China and the Pacific Ocean through Kazakstan.

How beneficial will the INSTC be when fully completed in 2019? According to estimates provided by some Indian experts, compared to the current route through the Suez Canal and the Mediterranean Sea, the INSTC is much shorter and cheaper. The INSTC can reduce both the time and cost of container delivery by 30 to 40%. From Nhava-Sheva port (Mumbai, India) the route by sea through the Suez Canal takes 45 to 60 days. The INSTC will take 25 to 30 days. In fact, the INSTC is 40% shorter in time and 30% cheaper.

But that is not the end of the story. Even now, before the INSTC has become fully operational, two shortcomings have already been noted. First, the Bandar Abbas port in Iran will rapidly become overburdened. Second, there are no linkages with Afghanistan. India and Iran are already planning an eastern leg of the INSTC to resolve both shortcomings. It may be discussed next week.

Putin's Genius

by Jeffrey Steinberg

March 14—Russia's President Putin has conducted a global flanking operation in Syria, aimed at bringing the Syrian tragedy to an end through the only means available. But he was simultaneously playing on the global stage—altering the political balance in Europe, boosting sane factions in Washington who understand the urgency of a revived U.S.-Russian partnership, creating a long-overdue wedge between Turkey's Erdogan regime and Turkey's NATO partners, boosting Russian-Chinese strategic collaboration, calling the Saudi bluff and bluster, and correcting some glaring flaws in Iran's strategic thinking.

Russias secret weapon: Vladimir Putin's genius. Putin is pictured here aboard the battlecruiser Pyotr Velikiy *during the Northern Fleet exercise in 2005.*

On March 5, the German magazine *Focus* published details of a leaked NATO report, acknowledging the effectiveness of the Russian military deployments in Syria, which have been vastly more successful against the Islamic State than the longer-running and larger U.S. and NATO military operations.

While the NATO paper was accurate in its characterization of the Russian operations, which began Sept. 30, 2015, a much more important truth was overlooked altogether.

Yes, the Russian Su-35 is the most advanced fighter jet in existence anywhere today. Yes, the Russians have capitalized on accurate and real-time on-the-ground intelligence to identify terrorist targets and strike them effectively. Yes, the Russians have been able to minimize civilian casualties and other collateral damage, reflecting a degree of training and care that is often missing from the Western deployments in Syria.

But the reality is that it was the genius of Russian President Vladimir Putin—who made the command decision to launch the Syrian operation at a critical moment, totally outflanking the United States and Brit-

ain, and other Western powers—which was the key to the potential victory. This factor of political genius was decisive in the turnaround in the entire Syrian situation.

Today, the second round of Geneva talks between the Syrian government and rebel factions backed by the United States, Saudi Arabia, Turkey, and other Gulf states, has begun. A two-week ceasefire has largely held, with a handful of daily violations, but with a tremendous decline in fighting, allowing humanitarian aid to get into parts of Syria that have been shut off for as long as five years. The United States and Russia are co-managing the ceasefire, through monitoring centers in Latakia, Syria, and Amman, Jordan. The Geneva talks have the unanimous backing of the United Nations Security Council through a joint Russian-American resolution.

It is almost an understatement that none of this would have been possible without President Putin's decision to take decisive action in Syria last summer.

Reports that Gen. Qasem Soleimani, the head of the Iranian Revolutionary Guard Corps' al-Quds Brigade, secretly flew to Moscow early last summer to meet personally with President Putin have been confirmed by well-placed Washington sources. Gen. Soleimani urged Putin to intervene to avert a collapse of the Syrian military and potentially of the Syrian government in Damascus.

There Is No Substitute for Victory

Prior to the Soleimani trip to Moscow, Russia had recently withdrawn 100 military intelligence advisers from Syria, because the Iranians and Hezbollah had effectively taken control of the fight against the Saudi- and Turkish-backed rebels, and were making some serious strategic mistakes. They were effectively ceding

The Distribution of Armed Forces in Syria, March 2016

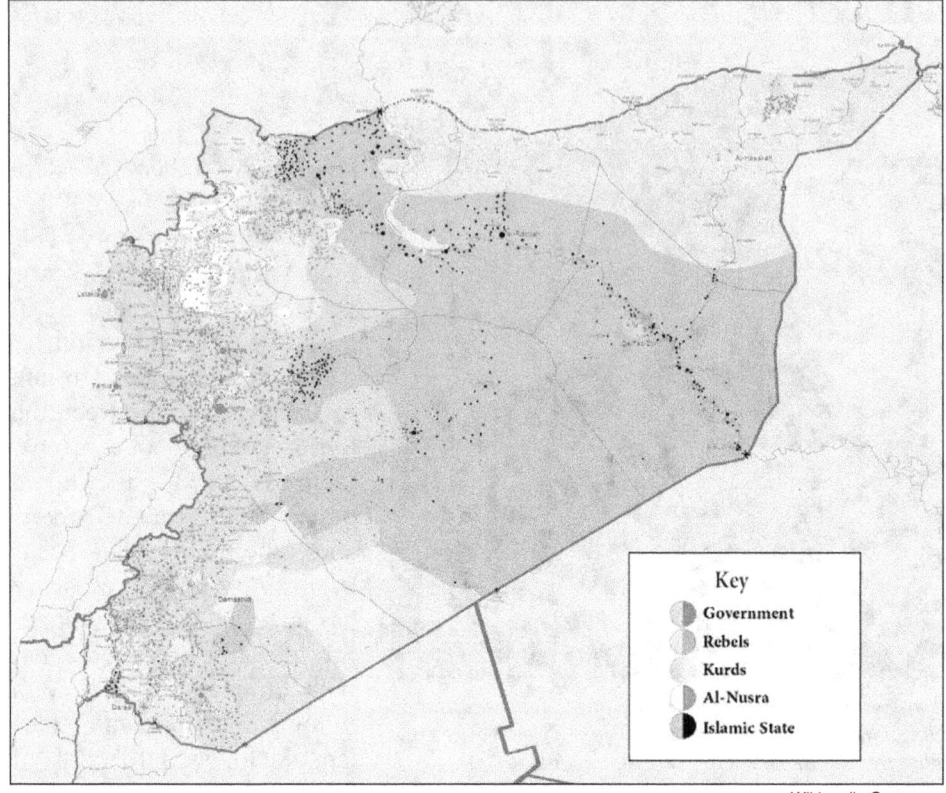

Key
- Government
- Rebels
- Kurds
- Al-Nusra
- Islamic State

Wikimedia Commons

major parts of the country to the foreign-backed anti-Assad fighters and were preparing to accept the reduction of the area of government control to Damascus and the mountain areas of Latakia province on the Mediterranean coast, where a majority of Alawites reside.

Putin understood that the fight was for all of Syria and anything short of a perspective of total victory was a losing proposition. The Russian deployment was premised on just such a total victory against all of the foreign-backed terrorists, not just the Islamic State and the al-Qaeda (Nusra Front) forces.

With that concept driving the entire Russian deployment, the Russians committed some of their newest, state-of-the-art military equipment, including the already mentioned Su-35 fighter jets, as well as S-400 air defense systems, which had never before been used in combat operations.

Putin also understood that the Russian intervention was a military-diplomatic strategic intervention. Unlike the United States, Britain, France, Saudi Arabia, and Turkey, Putin devised a top-down, integrated approach. When Putin or his Foreign Minister Sergei Lavrov declared that the Syrian war could not be won

on the battlefield, but had to be won through a diplomatic process, they were not just delivering empty phrases. They meant it, and they had a strategy for simultaneously creating the conditions for an end to the Syrian tragedy and for recapturing almost the entire territory of Syria, except for those areas temporarily in the hands of ISIS and Nusra.

Putin also knew that Western officials, with very few exceptions, would be blinded to the Russian flanking operations—on the battlefield and at the diplomatic table—by the hatred for the Russian President that permeated official circles in Washington, London, Paris, and even Berlin.

For months the American media fixated on the fact that the Russian/Syrian combined forces were not exclusively targeting ISIS and Nusra. They were conducting conventional warfare, aimed at cutting off the main roads leading to ISIS territory, cutting off the logistical lines running from NATO member Turkey into ISIS- and Nusra-controlled parts of northern Syria, and cutting the links between the Syrian and Iraqi territories held by ISIS.

The mainstream media joined key Obama White House officials in repeatedly denouncing Putin and the Russians for targeting Western-backed Syrian rebel forces, failing even to study the battle maps of the country to understand the Russian deployments.

It is in this domain—strategic thinking in depth—where Putin's genius, in stark contrast to the foolishness of the vast majority of political leaders and pundits in the West, stands out as the decisive factor to be understood.

The *Focus* magazine's leaking of the NATO document made clear that some Brussels military analysts have caught on to the fact that the Russians have conducted themselves professionally, have abided by the international laws of warfare, and have developed capabilities that far exceed those of NATO itself.

Putin has shown himself to be a grand strategist, and that is the ultimate message from the NATO document.

ACADEMICIAN MIKHAIL TITARENKO IN MEMORIAM

Visionary of Eurasian Cooperation

by Rachel Douglas

March 10—A man passed away on Feb. 25 2016, whose name the reader likely has never heard, although he changed your life. Academician Mikhail Titarenko, who died at the age of 81 after a lengthy illness, headed the Institute of Far Eastern Studies of the Russian Academy of Sciences (IFES RAS) from 1985 until last year.

Founder of the Schiller Institutes, Helga Zepp-La-Rouche wrote in a message of condolence to the late academician's colleagues, "If the world is pulled back from the abyss and a new paradigm brings about a new chapter in human history, it will be thanks to the strategic alliance between Russia and China, and Mikhail Titarenko has probably contributed more than anyone else for it to come into being."

Titarenko was, Zepp-LaRouche continued, "the perfect example of why the study and knowledge of other cultures is the basis for peace." He was one of the foremost intellectual authors of what has become the Eurasian development perspective of the New Silk Road, the Eurasian Land-bridge, and

the BRICS (the Brazil-Russia-India-China-South Africa group of countries).

Academician Titarenko became one of Russia's leading Sinologists during years when Chinese-Russian relations were rocky, to say the least. As a young graduate of Moscow State University in philosophy, he went in 1957 to study for two years at Beijing University, earning qualifications in Chinese language and philosophy. He studied not only socialist teachings, but also philosophy as taught by scholars of an older generation, such as Feng Youlan (1895-1990), who had reintroduced the study of all schools of ancient Chinese thought, and, in particular, the "neo-Confucianism" of Zhu Xi (1130-1200AD).

Following his studies, Titarenko's career coincided with the Sino-Soviet split, beginning in 1960. Despite intense economic cooperation in the 1950s, relations between the two countries deteriorated to the point of armed clashes on the Ussuri River in 1969. During these years, Titarenko was in the diplomatic service

IGNAT SOLOVEY/STRF.RU

Mikhail Leontyevich Titarenko was director of the Far East Institute of Russian Academy of Sciences (IFES RAS) from 1985 until last year. He was one of the foremost intellectual authors of Russian-Chinese cooperation, which has led to the present Eurasian development perspective characterized by the New Silk Road and the BRICS.

at the Soviet Consulate in Shanghai (1961-62) and the Embassy in Beijing (1963-65). He then worked for twenty years as a China expert at the Central Committee of the Communist Party of the Soviet Union, all the while pursuing his studies of China and earning advanced degrees.

He later supervised the production of a Russian encyclopedic dictionary of Chinese philosophy, and the five-volume *Encyclopedia of the Spiritual and Intellectual Culture of China.* In one of his last writings, the 2014 book *Russia and China: Strategic Partnership and the Challenges of Today,* Academician Titarenko termed the Russia-China strategic partnership in the Twenty-first Century "a tectonic shift" in the world.

The Strategic Triangle

Titarenko assumed leadership of the IFES RAS in 1985, on the eve of the beginnings of a turnaround in Chinese-Russian Relations. Though Soviet President Mikhail Gorbachov visited Beijing in 1989 and met with Chinese leader Deng Xiaoping, ending three decades of hostility, diplomatic contacts between the countries were sporadic in the 1990s after the collapse of the Soviet Union.

A visit to Russia by then-President Jiang Zemin in 1998 served as a keynote for coming changes. Arriving three months after the August 1998 financial crash in Russia, Jiang not only visited Moscow, but stopped at the science center of Akademgorodok in Novosibirsk. There Jiang spoke to the real Russia, pointing to Russian prowess in science and technology as a "shining beacon" of the "inexhaustible" human wisdom that makes possible the progress of mankind.

One month later while visiting New Delhi, Russian Prime Minister Yevgeni Primakov announced his initiative for the formation of a Russia-India-China "strategic triangle" in Eurasia. This step opened the door to greatly intensified bilateral and trilateral diplomacy among the great powers of the Eurasian continent, and to the formalization of the Shanghai Cooperation Organization (SCO) in 2001 and, ultimately, of BRICS. As the 2014 *EIR* Special Report *The New Silk Road Becomes the World Land-Bridge* put it, the collaboration of the Eurasian powers, proposed by Primakov, "came to life through a years-long sequence of three-way academic and diplomatic meet-

ings; after many turns in the road, the 'RIC' combination today is the core of the alliance called the BRICS."

Pages and pages of condolence messages on the IFES RAS website, in Chinese, English, and Russian, make clear that Mikhail Titarenko was a prime mover of this process. They can be read here: Perusing these messages from prominent scholars around the world provides a unique window into current history.

Prof. Manoranjan Mohanty of the Indian Institute of Chinese Studies wrote to the acting director of the IFES RAS, Dr. Sergei Luzyanin:

> The birth of the RIC (Russia-India-China) academic forum largely was the outcome of Professor Titarenko's initiative. It was he who had proposed the idea of cooperation among scholars and governments of India, China, and Russia in 1998 to the Institute of Chinese Studies, after which we took it up with the Chinese scholars who warmly responded to the proposal. That academic forum had inspired the meeting of the Foreign Ministers of RIC, leading to many high-level initiatives. On its efforts today BRICS has emerged as a globally significant force, playing a major role in restructuring of the international political economy. The RIC Academic Forum continues to meet alternately in the three countries, taking up crucial matters of peace, security and sustainable development. Having closely worked with Academician Titarenko on this multilateral initiative, I particularly remember his contribution to this process, his research-based writing on the subject and critical interventions on policy issues, his vision for creating a just and equitable world, in the making of which our three countries can play a significant role.

There are scores of such tributes on the IFES RAS site, from Russian Foreign Minister Sergei Lavrov and the Russian Ambassadors to China and India; from dozens of Chinese government officials and university scholars, the Chinese-Russian Friendship Society, China's national Anti-Terrorism Committee, and leading Chinese publications; from Korea, Vietnam, more from India, from institutes of the RAS and regional Russian universities, and a handful of American and European scholars.

Ambassador A.M. Kadakin, currently representing Russia in India, called Titarenko a "wise mentor" to several generations of Russian diplomats. Patriarch Kirill and Metropolitan Hilarion of the Russian Orthodox Church hailed his work on promoting the study of China's ancient culture in Russia, developing Chinese-Russian relations, and helping to revive the Orthodox Church in China, where it had a historical presence especially in the northeast.

My colleague Ramtanu Maitra of *EIR* wrote to the IFES that he "had the good fortune of meeting [Academician Titarenko] once in New Delhi in the late 1990s after Prime Minister Primakov had initiated the concept of developing the Russia-China-India triangle to stabilize the world in the post-Cold War days. Academician Titarenko was speaking at a conference which I, along with a few Indian friends, some of whom he knew, attended. On the side, discussing the world affairs, I was impressed not only about his understanding of the region, but his sincere goodwill about us all. I found him a man of great integrity, deeply opposed to geopolitics and conflicts."

Academician Titarenko's acquaintance with the Schiller Institute and Helga Zepp-LaRouche's campaign for the Eurasian Land-Bridge dates back to the mid-1990s, when his IFES colleagues were inspired by and publicized the Eurasian Land-Bridge concept and map, published in the *EIR* Special Report *The Eurasian Land-Bridge: The "New Silk Road" Locomotive for Worldwide Economic Development*. That report contained Zepp-LaRouche's address to the May 1996 Beijing International Symposium on Economic Development of the Regions along the New Euro-Asia Continental Bridge. In 1998, both she and Titarenko took part in the mobile Beijing International Symposium on Economic Development of the Regions along the New Euro-Asia Continental Bridge, in which, as participant Mary Burdman reported in *EIR* at the time, delegates from eight nations toured four Chinese cities to inspect the actual condi-

tions in the land-bridge region, and discuss its future development with national and regional Chinese leaders.

Titarenko fought for many years to overcome the prejudice of some in Russia who believed that Chinese continental bridge routes would be developed to the detriment of Russia's Trans-Siberian Railway. In 2011 he welcomed "Chinese interest in creating a transcontinental transport corridor from Southeast Asia to Europe through Russia." While noting that "China recognizes this corridor through Russia, and is even offering certain efforts to develop this project," Titarenko admonished Russian officials that the corridor would function only if Russia's own railways, including the Trans-Sib, were drastically modernized to handle fast container shipping.

The meeting of minds between Academician Titarenko and the Schiller Institute is well expressed by his 30th anniversary greeting to the institute in October 2014, and Zepp-LaRouche's condolence letter to Prof. Luzyanin.

Titarenko's Message
To the Schiller Institute

Dear Professor [Lyndon] LaRouche, Dear Helga:

On the occasion of the 30th anniversary of the Schiller Institute, please accept congratulations and best wishes from me personally, as well as from the many scholars at our Russian Academy of Sciences Institute of Far East Studies who know your work and activity.

For many years, you and your Institute have been doing exceptionally important work to shape a new international economic order and improve the world climate. The projects of the Schiller Institute, particularly those related to the Economic Belt of the Great Silk Road, the railway bridge in Eurasia, and the rehabilitation of the world financial system, are testimony to your profound insight, scientific honesty, and genuine civic and human courage.

In these current difficult times, we wish the Schiller Institute success in bringing your initiatives to fruition, as well as even more widespread recognition. To you personally, and all your colleagues: good health, redoubled creative energy, spiritual and intellectual well-being, and complete happiness!

Helga Zepp-LaRouche's Letter

Dear Professor Luzyanin,

From myself, my husband Lyndon LaRouche, and in the name of the international Schiller Institute, I would like to extend to you and all your colleagues at the Russian Academy of Sciences Institute of Far Eastern Studies deepest condolences on the death of Academician Mikhail Titarenko.

I have been privileged to know Academician Titarenko personally and to see him act as one of the intellectual fathers and most energetic organizers of the prospect of productive collaboration between Russia and China on the project of the New Silk Road and the Eurasian Landbridge. Today, the development of that cooperation, with its further extension through the "strategic triangle" China-India-Russia and then BRICS, gives mankind hope for a new, optimistic era of civilization, despite the tremendous danger of a new world war and economic collapse. If the world is pulled back from the abyss and a new paradigm brings about a new chapter in human history, it will be thanks to the strategic alliance between Russia and China, and Mikhail Titarenko has probably contributed more than anyone else for it to come into being.

During our 1998 "travel symposium" on the Eurasian Land-bridge, in which I had the honor and pleasure to participate with Academician Titarenko and Academician Dmitri Lvov, when we visited Beijing, Nanjing, Lianyungang, and Qinhuangdao, I came to appreciate what a powerful gift Mikhail Titarenko was giving to his own country and the world by using his profound knowledge of China to promote Chinese-Russian cooperation and build support for the Eurasian development perspective. He is the perfect example of why the study and knowledge of other cultures is the basis for peace. This journey will remain one of the outstanding memories of my life.

You have my best wishes for success in carrying forward the great work of Academician Titarenko. Please convey our deep sympathy to his family.

Every Day Counts
In Today's Showdown
To Save Civilization

That's why you need EIR's **Daily Alert Service**, a strategic overview compiled with the input of Lyndon LaRouche, and delivered to your email 5 days a week.

For example: On Jan. 7, EIR's Daily Alert featured the British hand behind the pattern of global provocations toward war. Of special note is British Intelligence's role in instigating the Saudi Kingdom's attempt to set off a Sunni-Shia war. This religious war has been the intent of British strategy since the Blair-Bush attack on Iraq in 2003.

We also uniquely update you regularly on the progress toward the release of the suppressed 28 pages of the Congressional Inquiry on 9/11, which would expose the Saudi role.

Every edition highlights the reality of the impending financial crash/bail-in policies that would realize the British goal of mass depopulation.

This is intelligence you need to act on, if we are going to survive as a nation and a species. Can you really afford to be without it?

THURSDAY, JANUARY 7, 2016

Volume 2, Number 97

EIR Daily Alert Service

P.O. Box 17390, Washington, DC 20041-0390

- British Crown Pushing War and Genocide in 2016
- Financial Mudslide Goes On; Monetarist Tyranny Gloats over Bail-Ins
- Moody's Downgrades Portugal's Novo Banco
- Puerto Rico's Default: It's Every Vulture for Himself
- Wide Glass-Steagall Debate Set Off Again by Sanders Speech
- MI6 Mouthpiece Evans-Pritchard Touts Persian Gulf Chaos
- North Korea Tests a Miniaturized Hydrogen Bomb
- Uighur Terrorists Found in Indonesia
- Foreign Investors Are Flocking In to China

EDITORIAL

British Crown Pushing War and Genocide in 2016

II. Road to Doom Under Barack Obama

The Death of the Trans-Atlantic World

by Robert Ingraham

Prologue

Dumbed-down Americans of today usually demand immediate, simple and *practical* solutions to the problems that the nation is facing. Serious political discourse has been replaced by Hollywood-style manipulation of the citizenry, resulting in a situation where a shallow-minded people are led around by the nose, with little thought or consideration given to the deeper issues of the day. Almost everything that most people think about the political process is a mere "opinion," created for them by the media and their masters on Wall Street—and then swallowed by a gullible public.

Eight years ago it was the media hype and hysteria around the "new hope" personified by Barack Obama which swept the country. Today it is the macho anti-establishment rhetoric of Donald Trump that has seemingly "come out of nowhere" to galvanize the population. Neither of these represent actual political phenomena; rather, today's trans-Atlantic culture is an Orwellian society, driven by manufactured popular opinion and contentless media posturing, all aimed at a malleable electorate which has lost the ability to think historically.

As a result, the critically important historical moment which America and the rest of the world now finds itself at is lost on the people of America. They simply have no idea of what is actually going on. They have no understanding of the profound importance of the choices now facing the nation; nay, they do not even know that such choices exist.

I. The British Empire

On Nov. 14, 1716 the great historical fighter and genius Gottfried Leibniz died. With him died all hope of reversing the process of the transformation of England into a stratified oligarchical state—into the headquarters for a new global empire.

For more than forty years, since his arrival in Paris in 1672, the towering personality of Leibniz had provided the leadership in Europe to resurrect the outlook of the fifteenth-century Florentine Renaissance. In science, philosophy, economics and diplomacy it was the mind of Leibniz which terrified the oligarchical rulers of Europe. It was Leibniz who revived and deepened the approach of Nicholas of Cusa, Filippo Brunelleschi, and Johannes Kepler, and who uncompromisingly defended and promulgated the true creative nature of the human species.

Between his arrival in Hannover in 1679 up until his death in 1716 Leibniz led a fight to establish England as a new center for republican and Renaissance values. This battle took on greater urgency after the Dutch invasion of 1688 and the subsequent efforts of the oligarchical Whig Junto to establish an oligarchical state and to clone the monetary and financial practices of Amsterdam onto London.

By no later than 1696 Leibniz was joined in this fight by Jonathan Swift, and after Leibniz helped sponsor the career of George Frideric Handel in England in 1710, that composer too became a leading ally in the fight against the growing ascendency of oligarchic culture and imperial practices in England.

The death of Queen Anne in 1714, followed two years later by the passing of Gottfried Leibniz, doomed these efforts within the British isles. The decisive victory of Britain in the Seven Years War and the provisions of the 1763 Treaty of Paris would establish the global hegemony of the British Empire as well as the relegation of continental Europe into a permanent subservience to that system of empire. Leibniz's efforts would live on, however, and be partially realized in 1776 and 1789 with the founding of the United States of America, a nation whose historic mission, as defined from the very beginning by Alexander Hamilton, was one of overthrowing the oligarchical power of Britain and promulgating a true human culture of progress and creativity. That mission, a sacred trust upon which the rest of humanity placed its hope, was never fully realized. By the Twentieth Century it was in retreat, and, as of 2016, it is a hair's-breadth away from vanishing forever.

Unless sufficient numbers of Americans, including those more intelligent individuals who inhabit influential positions within certain leading institutions, begin to recognize the true nature and the danger of the current crisis, the historic legacy of America is likely to be written for future generations as one of a great Shakespearean tragedy—of *what might have been*, of an unrealized potential for human development—a failure of the people of the nation to rise to the nec-

With the death of Queen Anne in 1714, the possibility of a Leibniz-influenced monarchy in Britain also died.

essary level of culture and moral courage. The story of America will become only one more example of an unsuccessful attempt to establish republican culture and one more defeated effort to resist British imperial power.

Destroying the Human Identity

In a public discussion with the LaRouche PAC Policy Committee on March 7, 2016, Lyndon LaRouche stated the following:

> Go back to the early Nineteenth Century, or into the Nineteenth Century, as such, before Bertrand Russell, and the Bertrand Russell effect is the thing that has destroyed the trans-Atlantic community. But Russell was evil. He was successfully evil. And so, therefore, you see the possibility and the implications. The development of the minds of the people, since the beginning of Bertrand Russell's appearance on the screen, has been one of continuing, not even evil, but that kind of force of destruction. People are becoming more and more stupid, more and more insane.[1]

In his Four Reports, particularly in his 1791 *Report on the Subject of Manufactures*, Alexander Hamilton defined not merely an economic policy for the United States, but a cultural outlook. For Hamilton, George Washington, and their allies, the concept of the nature of mankind was the Leibnizian view. The creative potential which exists within each human individual—this is what lies at the core of Hamilton's "economics." A future orientation of progress, scientific advancement, and the potential for an increasing perfectibility of human society defined America's mission in the eyes of Hamilton and his friends.

This was also the outlook of Gottfried Leibniz, and, as Leibniz fully understood, it is in the realm of defining the true nature of the human species that the actual warfare against the oligarchical system takes place.

As both Jason Ross[2] of the LaRouche Basement team and Dr. Ernie Shapiro of the Manhattan Project have recently demonstrated, the crucial point of attack taken by Leibniz in his fight with Isaac Newton is the nature of the human identity. For Leibniz, man is made in the image of the Creator, and the human mind possesses wondrous qualities of reason and creativity. For Newton, an employee of the ascendent empire faction in London, man is a beast, a wretch—incapable of understanding universal processes or unleashing the secrets of the universe through actual human discovery.

Through the efforts of the British Royal Society and individuals such as Jeremy Bentham, Adam Smith, John Stuart Mill, Charles Darwin, and Thomas Huxley, Newton's oligarchical view of human nature spread through both the Anglo-American world as well as into continental Europe during the entirety of the Nineteenth Century. This became the culture—as well as the hegemonic "scientific" method—of the entire trans-Atlantic world.

---

1. The full show is available at https://larouchepac.com/20160307/larouchepac-policy-committee-show-march-7-2016

2. See https://larouchepac.com/20160302/new-paradigm-show-leibniz-part-ii

In 1903, less than two years after the murder of U.S. President William McKinley, the British aristocrat Lord Bertrand Russell published *The Principles of Mathematics*. It is in this early work that Russell first argued his thesis that mathematics and logic are identical, and since, according to Russell, simple logic is the highest form of mental activity that the human species is capable of, it follows that all human mental processes can be defined in mathematical terms.[3] With this one writing, further developed in many subsequent works, Russell denies that human creativity exists. He denies the very essence of the human identity.

Russell's 1903 work was only the opening salvo. This oligarchical onslaught reached a crescendo with the assault against Einstein at the 1927 Fifth Solvay Conference and then escalated after World War II. The development of modern-day "Information Theory" is but one of the many effects of the supremacy of Russell's views within the scientific establishment. Russell denies true human discovery and the Renaissance method of hypothesis. The twentieth-century dominance of Russell's views within the scientific establishment and the intelligentsia of the trans-Atlantic world has led to a twenty-first-century culture of despair, pessimism, and hedonism.

This has been the intent of the degenerate oligarchy since the time of Leibniz. In the Twentieth Century this anti-human outlook came to dominate the trans-Atlantic world, corrupting all national cultures in Europe and the Americas. Despite sporadic resistance and counter-measures, trans-Atlantic culture is now fully subservient to the bestial outlook of Russell and his imperial friends.

II. The Impending Tragedy of the United States

For the entirety of its existence the United States has existed within a global environment dominated by the British Empire. America never fully succeeded in fulfilling its *raison d'être*—to destroy the power and outlook of the British Empire. Victories have been won,

Library of Congress

Turning point, 1901: U.S. President William McKinley is killed by a British-steered assassin to put Anglophile Vice President Teddy Roosevelt in the driver's seat. Overnight, with the help of the media, the British went from being our historic enemy to our dearest friend. Teddy Roosevelt corresponded secretly with King Edward VII. In the drawing, Leon Czolgosz, an anarchist influenced by Emma Goldman, shoots McKinley in a receiving line with a revolver wrapped in a handkerchief.

but the power and control of the British Empire has never been broken. The death of Hamilton shattered the initial American effort, and after the election of Thomas Jefferson in 1800, the vision and intent of the first Washington Administration became a minority view throughout most of the subsequent history of America. The ever-weakening republican impulse was fighting within a global environment controlled by Britain.

The number of truly great U.S. Presidents—Washington, Quincy Adams, Lincoln, Franklin Roosevelt—can be counted on the fingers of one hand. A small handful of others, including Grant, McKinley, Kennedy, and Reagan also demonstrated admirable courage in fighting for the American republican outlook. Almost all of the rest have been worthless, and more than a few outright scoundrels and traitors.

After 1900 things became much worse, as the culture of America was perverted and degraded and the true American identity began to vanish. Since then there have been four crucial turning points, each of which greatly worsened the situation inside the United States:

- 1901—The assassination of William McKinley. This act brought to a sudden end the 1861-1901 Lincoln Era. The Teddy Roosevelt presidency, com-

3. See http://larouchepub.com/other/2016/4305russell_made_us_stupid.html

Turning point, 1944-1945: Harry S Truman becomes President at Franklin D. Roosevelt's death on April 12, 1945, and supports the FBI takeover of the country, under way since 1944. In this 1950 photo, Truman smiles at FBI Director J. Edgar Hoover at the National Crime Conference in Washington, as Attorney General Howard McGrath looks on.

Turning point, 1986-1989: The collaboration between Lyndon LaRouche and President Ronald Reagan around the Strategic Defense Initiative is defeated, and LaRouche is framed and imprisoned in 1989. The LaRouche-Reagan collaboration was the last significant chance to reverse the pro-imperial trend in the United States. Here, LaRouche and Reagan at a 1980 candidates debate in Concord, N.H.

bined with the early twentieth-century role of Bertrand Russell, initiated the process of assimilating the United States into the practices, culture, philosophy and scientific methodology of the British Empire.

- The 1944-1945 turning point in the United States, including the FBI-orchestrated right-wing turn in America, the death of Franklin Roosevelt, and the social and strategic counter-revolution carried out under Harry Truman. These developments resulted in the full integration of the United States into the British-controlled trans-Atlantic system—culturally, economically, and geopolitically.

- The defeat of the 1980-86 collaboration between Lyndon LaRouche and Ronald Reagan around the Strategic Defense Initiative and the subsequent imprisonment of LaRouche in 1989. This destroyed the last significant opportunity to reverse the post-1945 pro-imperial trend within the United States.

- The period from 2001 to the present, inclusive of the entirety of the presidencies of George W. Bush and Barack Obama. These 15 years have witnessed an unprecedented destruction of America's productive capabilities, combined with a devastating intellectual, cultural and moral degeneracy, which now poses the question of whether the nation can continue to exist in its current form.

Turning point, 2001 to present: The presidencies of George W. Bush and Barack Obama have witnessed an unprecedented destruction of America's creative and productive capabilities. Here, President Obama jokes with George W. Bush aboard Air Force One before departure for South Africa, Dec. 9, 2013.

The current trans-Atlantic reality was not always so. John Quincy Adams' actions on behalf of a "Community of Principle" among nations, Abraham Lincoln's battle with the British-sponsored slave system of the Confederacy and the late nineteenth-century initiatives of James Blaine and William McKinley against the British Empire are all representative of the positive thread that runs through American history. But McKinley was murdered one hundred fifteen years ago, and except for the twelve-year presidency of Franklin Roosevelt, this recent era of more than one century has been characterized by the steady absorption of the United States into the policies and cultural outlook of the trans-Atlantic world.

We now find ourselves in a situation where the once-productive economy of the United States is a rubble heap. Our space program has been almost eliminated. The banking and financial system only continues to exist through outlandish and unsustainable gambling methods, ready to come crashing down at any moment. Most Americans have now joined with the residents of Britain and continental Europe in hysterical opposition to the development of nuclear power, perhaps the clearest example of the breakdown of cognitive abilities within the population. The educational system no longer works, and tens of millions, particular among the youth, clamor for the legalization of "recreational" drugs. A bestial view of mankind has become the dominant cultural matrix.

This is not sustainable. This is the death of our national culture. This is a tragedy on the real-world stage, as everything which was established in 1775-1789 is about to be lost.

A seismic realignment of human affairs, as unstoppable as the Fifth-century self-destruction of the Roman Empire, is already underway. America must ally with Russia and China against the imperial interests of London and Wall Street. Here, the Ruins of the Forum *(1742) by Eighteenth-century Italian master Canaletto.*

III. The End of the trans-Atlantic World

One of the more despicable features of current trans-Atlantic culture is a Euro-centric or Western-centric view of the world. Many Europeans like to pride themselves that they are not as stupid as Americans, that they are more knowledgeable about world affairs, but the issue here is not knowledge but chauvinism. Almost all Americans *and* Europeans have an ingrained cultural outlook of a trans-Atlantic-centered world view. European culture, of which the United States is an offshoot, is accepted as the most advanced in human history. Lip service is paid to the equality of all human beings, but it is quietly understood that Europe and America were the creators of modern art, science, and music. All other cultures, all other nations, although perhaps interesting, are inferior.

This outlook goes beyond the cultural realm into the arena of geopolitics and power. Beginning with the sixteenth-century colonial expeditions of Spain and Portugal, and continuing up to the present day, the trans-Atlantic nations have insisted that it is their right to run the world. Particularly, beginning with the establishment of the British Empire in 1763, and continuing through all of the Nineteenth Century and into World

War II, the vast majority of the peoples of the world were reduced to the status of colonial subjects of the European powers. This lasted for centuries.

That legacy, ingrained into trans-Atlantic culture, has led to a type of arrogance which one sees today in Barack Obama or in the reactions of Angela Merkel and other European leaders to the recent rational measures taken by Vladimir Putin. The attitude is simply, "We must be obeyed." This arrogance of power is now disintegrating, and it is soon to be "gone with the wind." The way in which the world has operated for the past three centuries is about to undergo a radical transformation. A seismic realignment of human affairs, as unstoppable as the self-destruction of the fifth-century Roman Empire, is already underway. The reality is that in the decades ahead Europe will increasingly be relegated to the fringes of the economic and scientific power emerging out of Asia.

A Dying Society

Every single nation in Western and Central Europe has a birth rate below replacement levels. As a people they are willing themselves out of existence. In order for a society to reproduce itself it is necessary for every woman of child-bearing age to bear, on average, 2.1 children. Every European nation, with the singular exception of Putin's Russia, is below that. Germany, Italy, Austria, and Switzerland are among the lowest in the world in birth rates. In southern and eastern Europe, where the effects of economic looting by the European Union have been the most brutal, birth rates have dropped below 1.3 per adult woman. If this continues the population there will be cut in half in just 45 years. In Italy, many cities, such as Milan and Bologna recorded rates lower than 1.0, which are the lowest birth-rates in the entire world.

This process of societal suicide has been accompanied by a dramatic collapse of culture.

Europeans, even 20 to 30 years ago, prided themselves on a vibrant classical music tradition, including not just premier orchestra and opera houses, but, far more important, a classical tradition in families, neighborhoods, the churches, and the schools. The German phenomenon of *musikabends* is paradigmatic of this tradition. Today, much of this is gone, vanished, and only sustained by a dwindling number of participants. And for many of the opera and concert-goers in Paris, Berlin, Vienna, and Milan—they have lost the ability to morally distinguish classical cul-

ture from the hegemonic bestial pop musical culture. What the music of Mozart, Bach, and Beethoven tells us about the true nature of the human mind, the human soul and the human identity is struggling to survive.

The United States has not been immune to the effects of this deep cultural pessimism. Six years into the presidency of George W. Bush, in 2007, U.S. births dropped below replacement level for the first time in the nation's history. By 2014 a study by the Centers for Disease Control reported that an American woman will give birth to an average of 1.88 children over her lifetime, a record low in American history

A Sudden Change

During the same discussion with the LaRouche PAC Policy Committee cited above, Lyndon LaRouche had the following to say:

Everything has changed. Everything that was understood beforehand, is no longer true. And we get intimations of that, as well as direct observations. And this is really something. We are at the point where the entire U.S. system is on the verge of a general collapse. That's what's on now. That's the situation. That's the reality. And there's no hope, there's no hope that under the present programs, that the U.S. system will able to continue to operate in its customary way. It's about ready to collapse. And that's what the general condition is.

And so what they're trying to do is cover up this fact, that there is no solution available for the entire economy. The entire economy is vulnerable. It could disintegrate very rapidly. And the warnings were given beforehand, even years beforehand. And we've come to a point, they're still doing the same old stupid thing. And it's worse than ever before.

So, you're in a situation where we cannot be secure in any assumption about what the next situation is going to be, because there can be different kinds of reactions to what this crisis, which is coming down on us. It can be, some people can handle it, some people can deal with it, Some people could respond in a rational way....

So, we're working on an enigma, of which

we have certain signs of possibility. That's what we have.

On the surface we can say that the errors of the United States, its characteristic, you could talk about various parts of Europe, their follies, and characteristics, they are all there. But the question is, where are the solutions found?

The solutions are found in Putin, who's a leader, China, a leader, and other nations which are being teased into that category. They're not into it. I mean, India is not into that category, it's on the edge of it. It's on the edge of the possibility of it. And other parts of the area, there are some that could become something.

It's the end of the old system. It needs to be replaced. It can be done. It's dangerous. Don't lose your nerve.

The British imperial system has reached the terminus of its quarter-millennium existence. It is bankrupt, economically ruined, and morally degenerate. If America remains locked into the axioms of the trans-Atlantic world, it will go down with it. Nothing can prevent that.

What is required is a shift. Everything doesn't have to happen at once. The Florentine Renaissance wasn't created in one day. But any hope for the future does depend an a decision being made, and that decision must be made by a growing number of Americans as well as leaders within the nation's establishment. America must ally with Russia and China against the interests of London and Wall Street. We must cut the trans-Atlantic system loose. This means shutting down the practices of Wall Street, permanently closing all of the hedge funds and other speculative institutions, and initiating economic reconstruction.

Again, none of this can be fully realized in one day or one week, but the decision to act can be instantaneous. As Lyndon LaRouche stated above, we live in a very dangerous world. The shift required to see our way through this danger is to simply offer a hand of friendship to Russia and China—to say, "We no longer are bound by our traditional ties with Britain and Europe. We want to work with you to build a better world." An obvious place to start would be in full collaboration on a crash space program. That decision will change everything.

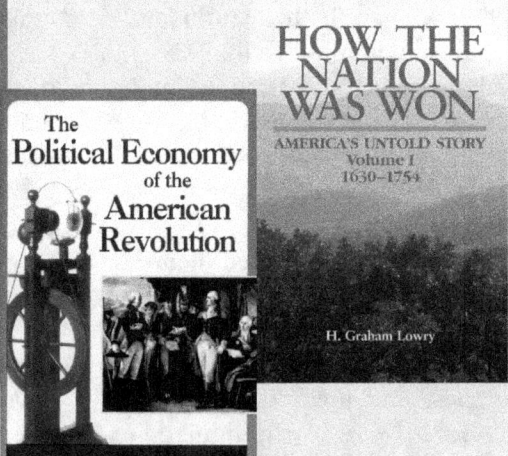

THE EUROPEAN CENTRAL BANK PUMPS MONEY

Bankrupt the Speculators, Not the Savers!

by Helga Zepp-LaRouche

March 11—The European Central Bank's (ECB) decision to set interest rates at zero, to charge negative interest rates for deposits, thus actually giving banks the money to take out ECB credit, as well as to raise its monthly amount of bond purchases from 60 to 80 billion euros, means only one thing: The trans-Atlantic financial system is hopelessly bankrupt. We are standing on the edge of a total collapse, and it is absolutely inexcusable for governments to allow such a system based on a deceitful hoax to be propped up even one day longer. The casino economy of the mega-speculators must immediately be shut down and replaced by a strict Glass-Steagall banking separation system! There is a solution, but it demands a dramatic turn away from the current neo-liberal model and a return to the real economy and economic development.

ECB head Mario Draghi, a former director at Goldman Sachs, has launched a total assault on German savers, savings banks, and small and medium-sized enterprises. Thus he has whipped out the very last card in the rigged poker game which the trans-Atlantic banking system turned itself into a long time ago. Now it's finished; they've shot their wad; at any moment the sudden death of the financial system could occur. It would throw us immediately in chaos.

An exaggeration? Here are the reactions of various economists and experts:

- Jürgen Stark, former chief economist of the ECB: "It's all going to

end in chaos. The ECB is going beyond its mandate and destroying public trust in the institution."
- Hans-Werner Sinn, president of the Ifo Institute for Economic Research and a member of the Chancellor's economic advisory council: "This is illicit subsidizing to support the zombie banks and countries threatened with bankruptcy."
- Clemens Fuest, President of the Center for European Economic Research as well as a member of the economic advisory council at the German Ministry of Finance: "The ECB has shot its wad."
- Wolfgang Gerke, President of the Bavarian Financial Center: This is "a frontal assault on all savers."
- Michael Kemmer, chief executive officer of the banking association: This is "poison."
- Anton Börner, President of the export association

Jürgen Stark, a former chief economist of the European Central Bank, reacts to its latest decisions: "Its all going to end in chaos."

Otmar Issing, another former economist of the European Central Bank, reacts: "Suicide from fear of death."

The monetarist paradigm is producing fascist movements, such as that of Donald Trump in the United States and Alternative für Deutschland *in Germany. Here, a demonstration of 40,000 organized by the xenophobic, right-wing Pegida movement in Dresden, Germany.*

BGA: "This is a gigantic redistribution from the North to the South. Politically, it carries a huge explosive charge, when put it together with the refugee crisis. It is highly dangerous."

- Wolfgang Steiger, General Secretary of the Christian Democratic Union's Economic Council: "The policy of cheap money destroys confidence. When the medicine is wrong, it doesn't help to raise the dose."
- Otmar Issing, former chief economist of the ECB: "Suicide from fear of death."
- Professor Richard Werner, Southampton University: The ECB's policy will probably destroy half of the 1,500 savings banks and cooperatives in Germany: "We've learned nothing from the financial crisis. The sooner there's a revolt in Germany, the better."

The Policy Has Failed

But the failure of the European Monetary Union and the "rescue package" for the banks after the collapse of Lehman Brothers in 2008 is not the only policy failure of the European Union. The images of refugees at the Greek-Macedonian border are the reflection of the total inhumanity of the EU, which knows neither union nor solidarity, and whose "values" certainly have nothing to do with Europe's humanist tradition.

The line which Chancellor Merkel has apparently oriented to—namely, focussing everything on securing the EU's external borders through helping Frontex and an arrangement with Turkey—is just as unenforceable as it is irresponsible. You need only look at the map of Europe to see that desperate people who are fighting for survival, will always find a way to cross borders. The idea of solving the refugee crisis with the help of Turkey is downright absurd.

In contrast to the naïveté and pragmatism of Merkel's help for Turkish President Erdogan in his recent election and of her current policy, two former U.S. ambassadors to Turkey, under Presidents Bush senior and junior, Morton Abramowitz and Eric Edelman, describe the Erdogan regime as one which is authoritarian, collapsing economically, and waging a civil war against its own people. Moreover, the UN High Commissioner for Human Rights, Zeid Ra'ad al-Hussein, called the planned mass deportation of refugees from Greece illegal. At the UN Human Rights Council in Geneva, he stated that border restrictions that do not determine the circumstances of each individual violate international and European law.

But it's not only that: The Turkish government's support for the ISIS terrorist organization—and thus, one of the causes of the refugee crisis—has been sufficiently documented by various intelligence services and media. Given that state of affairs, to become dependent on the Turkish regime is more than amateurish; it is irresponsible.

Responsible politicians in the so-called West, and especially in Germany, must recognize that they are responsible for this gigantic policy failure; that they have totally bungled every opportunity that has come up since the fall of the wall in 1989 to build a truly peaceful world order for the Twenty-first Century; and that the blatant failure of their policy will endure as their historical legacy—provided there actually is a history.

The very fact that there is such a phenomenon as Donald Trump in the United States, whom the former Labor Secretary under the Clinton Administration Robert Reich has correctly likened to the fascists of the 1930s, or as the *Alternative für Deutschland* party, which plays to the lowest impulses of the population, is the result of the policies of the established parties. The neo-liberal, monetarist paradigm which puts profit for the greedy far above the general welfare, has produced the monster, which now fills the future with alarming question marks.

The Way Out

Despite everything, there's no reason to despair. There is a way out of the crisis. It is the tested policy of Franklin D. Roosevelt, who in 1933 created the model which can end the casino economy with the Glass-Steagall Act. And above all, there is the offer by China to overcome the current financial and economic crisis by expanding the New Silk road on the basis of "win-win" cooperation. The *only* way to overcome the refugee crisis is through large-scale economic development of Southwest Asia and Africa, so that the people who are now fleeing to us due to war and starvation, have a perspective for reconstructing and developing their own homelands. China has offered this cooperation, and Russian President Putin has created the prerequisites for a political and economic solution through his military intervention in Syria.

The strategic constellation exists for cooperation with China, Russia, the BRICS nations and the alternative financial institutions which they have created—such as the Asian International Investment Bank (AIIB), the New Development Bank (NDB BRICS), the Silk Road Fund, and so forth. Our ability to get out of this existential crisis will decisively depend upon whether enough people and institutions are able to recognize the axiomatic basis for the current policy failures, and consciously determine to bring about a new paradigm.

Solutions for this complex crisis can obviously not be found on either local or national levels. The new paradigm must proceed from the common aims of mankind, and create a real perspective for all nations on the planet. As Chinese President Xi Jinping expressed it in his speech before the United Nations in September 2015, and as an old Chinese proverb goes: "The greatest ideal is to create a world truly shared by all."

This proverb is commonly known among all the Chinese, and especially all the young people in the country. We should quickly adopt it as our own.